Religion

FELIPE FERNÁNDEZ-ARMESTO

PHŒNIX

A PHOENIX PAPERBACK

First published in Great Britain in 1997 by
Phoenix, a division of the Orion Publishing Group Ltd
Orion House
5 Upper Saint Martin's Lane
London, WC2H 9EA

A CIP catalogue record for this book is available
from the British Library.

ISBN 0 297 81895 3 ✓

Typeset by SetSystems Ltd, Saffron Walden
Set in 9/13.5 Stone Serif
Printed in Great Britain by
Clays Ltd, St Ives plc.

PREDICTIONS

Contents

Introduction

'All the old religions are discredited' in the fourth millennium, as Arthur C. Clarke imagines it. Instead, there are immortals of 'pure-energy' who preside over our descendants' world from another, unseen universe. Divinity, it seems, is hard to get rid of and, while religions come and go, religious tics are ineradicable. God is dead: long live the gods!

It used to be fashionable to predict the end of religion. It would be replaced by earth-bound realism, perhaps, critical reason, practical utility, dialectical materialism, scientific humanism or unsentimental science. Nietzsche thought faith was a pathological aberration of which willpower would cure us, Lenin that it could be tolerated as a doomed anachronism. H. G. Wells assumed it would be superseded by progress, like earlier, cruder forms of superstition and magic. Bertrand Russell thought 'as near as possible to certainty' that it was false.

So far, however, ancient faiths have outfaced all proposed successors. In each of the last five centuries the critics of old religions have ended up inventing new ones. Almost all the 'atheists' deplored by divines in the sixteenth and seventeenth centuries turn out, on close examination, to have been something else – usually deists or fideists, sometimes pantheists or merely heretics. More recent attempts to break out of religion have slightly shifted its confines. The eighteenth-century escape-route led to the cult of the Supreme Being, erected alongside the guillotine as a memorial of perverted reason. Modern pragmatists sometimes think they have a non-religious answer to fundamental questions like 'What is truth?' and 'What is right?' – but William James, the most effective spokesman for pragmatism, used it to justify a feeble form of Christianity. Other refugees from faith have turned their disbelief into religion of another sort. Humanists made a god of man. Communists replaced God with equally potent, equally transcendent History. Scientists substituted godlike evolution for discarded providence. Most predictions are no longer of a religionless world, merely of a world with new religions. Religions come and go – but, mostly, they come and stay, changing all the time but never transforming religion itself out of existence.

We want to know now whether traditionally recognizable religions can go on resisting erosion and attack and how, meanwhile, the process will change them. By religion I mean a system of belief, shared in a framework of social relationships, which must include what Schleiermacher, the 'father of modern Protestantism', called 'a sense of and taste for the infinite and eternal'. For purposes of the present essay, and for reasons which will be explained in a moment, I exclude what I call quasi-religions and para-religions, including many influential superstitions, cults and movements, because, despite religious pretensions, they do not nourish a sense of transcendence which genuinely reaches for the infinite and eternal.

To religion in this traditional sense, there are four sources of threat. Secularism could still win the cosmic struggle: science might yet gut the wonder out of creation, and human yearning could be glutted by the material satisfactions of life. Further or alternatively, religion could starve in the barren mental landscape constructed by postmodern diffidence. Meanwhile, religious revival favours para-religious sects and cults or individual obsessions more than mainstream religion: this raises the fear that religious traditions will fragment into something unrecognizable, retreat into mental ghettos or dematerialize in cyberspace. Finally, new forms of syncretism could transmute religion into a kind of secular therapy, or a range of designer-label faiths, or a form of fantasy for the intellectually challenged: some 'Next Church' movements and 'prosperity gospels', for instance, are so immersed in worldliness as to be unrecognizable as religions. On some current trends, therefore, the chances are that religion will wither or atrophy or merge with the world or become a freakish fringe.

2

This essay is a short attempt to dismiss those dangers and to predict and explain the inexhaustible appeal of religion in any kind of realistically imaginable future. Religions are their own worst enemies. They have more to fear from each other than, say, from science. They are threatened less by secular rivals than by their own infidelity to their proper objectives. Society, fortunately for them, is changing in their favour.

Chapter 1
The Apes of Faith

It is Sunday afternoon and the anthropologist from another galaxy is hovering over Earth.

He would have got here this morning if the complexities of space–time had allowed. For his aim is to test a colleague's earlier fieldwork by replicating, as nearly as possible, its exact conditions. While observing earthlings at worship, he hopes to discover how accurately their religion has been reported or how it has changed since the last observations were made.

He heads for Madrid, where, his files tell him, people are sure to be going to church in large numbers. He has no difficulty in identifying a vast, open-air basilica, thronged by thousands of pilgrims who wear the white-and-purple stoles which, his sources confirm, are part of the standard ritual garb. The congregation gathers in self-induced ecstasy, swaying in unison, singing out repetitive incantations. The priests arrive – two teams of priests, each in an obviously symbolic colour: the white of celestial purity, the red of blood-sacrifice and mephitic fire. This is obviously a dualist religion.

The psychomachia – the symbolic struggle of good and evil – is enacted in a grassy sanctuary in the middle of the basilica. A symbol which roughly reproduces the form of the planet is made to descry lines, arcs and curves across the sanctuary, and to oscillate wildly between the zones of earth and heaven, in apparently simultaneous mimesis of the cosmic and moral courses of the world. From time to time it seems to be engulfed in a net that resembles the maw of some divine creature with the power to destroy creation; but it is always mercifully regurgitated. The world is spared, disgorged, and the symbolic struggle is resumed.

The ball which represents the world is so sacred that not

even the priests can normally touch it with their hands, except for two pontiffs of the highest order, who guard the extremities of the holy sward and wear garb of distinctive colours. The only exception admitted is when the ball becomes defiled by bouncing or flying outside the boundaries of the inner enclosure. A priest then reconsecrates it by lifting it above his head and flinging it into the cosmic fray with a gesture evocative of a thunderbolt. Another priest in black, who seems to represent the interventions of chaos, blows a shrill note on a tiny pipe at random intervals and causes the earth-symbol to be shifted from place to place, patternlessly, around the inner temple.

At first the anthropologist is puzzled by the freedom with which the priests use their feet to touch the ball and direct its motions. He knows that the feet are not much revered by earthlings, compared with their heads, which are also allowed to touch the ball (and which they usually treat with vanity unjustified by their ugliness). The obvious interpretation suddenly strikes him. The status of feet is a function of their closeness to the earth, for in locomotion, as the earthlings oddly practise it, the feet are always in contact with the surface of the planet. This is a telluric religion and only the most privileged limbs can touch the earth-symbol.

In 1967, José Luis Sampedro, one of the best Spanish writers of recent times, imagined this device of football-as-rite (which I have adapted with modifications) to satirize secularism and to lampoon academic anthropology. It discloses or suggests a deeper truth: secular life imitates religion. The similarities in football's case have surely not been consciously aped. There are, however, secular ideologies and institutions which adopt rituals, vaunt transcendent explanations, make moral claims, focus loyalties, mobilize identities and create quasi-priesthoods. Some are billed as alternatives or successors to religion.

Marxism and Nazism have been incandescent recent cases, now burnt out. Both were presented by their adherents as 'scientific' prescriptions which made religion dispensable. Yet both were quasi-religions which borrowed heavily from religious tradition. They were alike in many other respects, as rival extremisms always are – as close as the ends of a horseshoe. Along one dimension, there was a long way between them, yet they almost touched. They were united against religion and united in imitation of it.

They replaced God with history but both saw the course of the world as charted by an impersonal, dynamic force, of which individual lives are the plaything. They offered human sacrifices to history, speeding her purposes by immolating profane races and classes. They adopted the framework and imagery of Christian millenarianism, promising the fulfilment of history in a 'classless society' or a 'thousand-year Reich', after a kind of armageddon. They had their well-orchestrated liturgies, their shrines and sanctuaries, their icons and saints, their processions and ecstasies, their hymns and chants. Both demanded irrational assent from their followers – submission to the infallibility of the Führer or to the scriptures of Marx. Both had their theological squabbles, as Internationals splintered like sects and heretics of the Strasser front were purged. Mikhail Tukhaveski, best of the generals of the first Red Army, dreamed of 'returning to our Slav gods'. Nazis fantasized about restoring ancient folk-paganism and turned *Heimschutz* into a mystic quest, leading through stone circles to Wewelsburg Castle, where, Himmler believed, ley-lines met at the centre of Germany and the world.

Marxism and Nazism were crude, looking-glass images of religion. Real religion has seen both off. But we still live in societies with worldly priorities, daunting anxieties, susceptibility to charisma and hunger for 'final solutions'. Some popular secular ideologies already seem to be practising in front of the mirror. Environmentalism sidles into earth-worship. On its sillier edge, feminism erects the mother of all idols and advocates the idiocies of 'Goddess-consciousness'. Mad capitalists celebrate their own millennium: the 'end of history' in a universal triumph of Chicago-style libertarianism. There is a kind of militant atheism which is religious in its fervour. There are scientists who worship Science, replace providence with the selfish gene and venerate Darwin as their prophet. All these threaten to be the post-religions of the future. If past form is anything to go by, as with Marxism and Nazism, real religion will outlive them.

A book on the future of religion might embrace these

movements and the weaker imitations which you can see competing with religion today. The cults of celebrities, for instance, generate worship-like hysteria, commerce in icons and the imitation of unsuitable saints. Veneration of historic communities has, for those who belong to them, some of the attractions of life in a sect, nourishing the exclusive identity of chosen people. Rites of business turn corporations into communions and, especially in the context of campaigns to 'motivate' sales, copy the conventions and aspire to the atmosphere of evangelical revivalism.

The difference between religion and business is sometimes hard to define. The 'Church' of Scientology claims to be a religion and has some of the trappings of one, but the law in some countries classes it as a business on the grounds that its purpose is to sell the works and gimcrack inventions of its founder. Is 'Exegesis' – a seminar-network devoted to the 'business of transformation and the transformation of business' by therapies which target the spirit – a business or a religion? The cult founded by the Baghwan Shree Rajneesh and made familiar by its adherents' orange robes offers 'Awareness courses' to those it calls 'clients' as well as rituals for believers.

This essay, however, is about the future of religion as traditionally defined, and the quasi-religions have an important place in it only in two respects: as reminders of the continuing power of real faith to attract imitators, and as rivals which – in some people's hopes or fears – will sap its appeal.

For similar reasons, renascent and newly contrived superstitions – for all their importance nowadays – have to be confined to the same margin as quasi-religions, even when they acquire sophisticated organizations. By superstitions, I mean irrational beliefs which represent defences against hostile nature rather than a religious commitment to the infinite and eternal, though they may add what some other imitations of religion lack: a celebration of the rationally imperceptible. Astrology, for instance, invests astral influences with the powers of providence. Flying-saucer freaks and corn-circle cranks are seeking 'encounters' with the kind of controlling intelligence which real religions leave to God. From elves to

7

'aliens', all the commonest delusions of superstition are emanations from a species afraid to be alone in the universe.

Nowadays there is almost no such thing as harmless superstition. Instant communications make every nerd a potential neophyte. For most dabblers, astrology and tarot are parlour pranks; but the scale on which they are trusted and the money they make suggest their potential social influence is enormous. The same was true of 'table-turning' in the past and the history of Spiritualism is a useful object-lesson. It started in a middle-class household in small-town, upstate New York, in 1848, where two young sisters heard rappings which their mother interpreted as messages from the spirit of a murder victim. More mediums, most of whom were women of otherwise unmarketable talents, discovered similar gifts. There was a time – not certainly over until the 1930s – when Spiritualism threatened to become one of the routine rituals of polite society in the West, perhaps because it responded to trivial anxieties which crowd great questions out of most people's minds. For Spiritualists favoured simpletons as mediums – partly as proof against charges of charlatanism. In consequence, messages from the other side were dominated by humdrum news of the loved ones' health and hobbies and petty friendships and jealousies.

This example is worrying for anyone who wants reasonable religion to survive today's weird fashions in belief. If Spiritualism could enjoy such a triumph how much more are equivalent forms of modern silliness likely to thrive, with information micro-technology at their command. Astrology is the starting-point of the 'New Age' movement, which seems lightly organized, if at all, but which is united by a common focus, a common literature and a certain wild consistency. The 'dawn of Aquarius' irradiates all its maunderings: the doctrine that the astral prominence of the constellation of Pisces is gradually being replaced, after about 2,000 years. New Age expectations defy critical intelligence. The movement is a sump into which every kind of fashionable superstition drains. It is hard to credit many people with belief in much of it – but even a little is brain-rotting. It taints the respectably suprarational by contagion and puts coins in the charlatans' slots.

Its success is an index of spiritual malaise: it responds craving for wonder and fervour which religion ought to able to supply. Superstition and secular quasi-religions have no part in an essay on the future of religion; but they may leave religion with no role in life.

Yet profane movements' habits of self-sacralization help to make some students of the subject suspect that religion is an inescapable part of being human. We can claim to reject it as individuals but in societies we really seem unable to do without it. At least, so it is often said, none of our human societies has managed so far. The ocean of collective experience is unnavigable without mast and sail and flag, which religion seems satisfactorily – perhaps uniquely – able to provide. Religions are ways of encoding inherited wisdom, without which the species would not be truly itself. Religious behaviour is part of the skeleton of culture which cannot be filleted without collapse.

This argument is useless except, perhaps, to doom religions to the fall which follows complacency. For, if religion were really necessary, what would make it so? It cannot be instinct, because there are some people who are genuinely irreligious. It cannot be social evolution, for that would be logically unsatisfactory – it would imply a stage or state of society prior to the need for religion. The view that religion is inescapable or in some sense natural is based on the fallacy that it is universal. On the contrary, it seems to me, religion properly understood – in terms which encompass belief and an active, lively sense of human responsibilities that transcend this world – is a relatively rare state of man. There never was an 'age of faith'. Most people, for most of history, have been indifferent to transcendence, unmindful of the eternal, neglectful of the infinite and content or obliged to wallow in worldly priorities. Quasi-religions ape only external habits that arise from a life of faith. If – for one reason above all others – it is unconvincing to suppose that religion is over, it is because, so far, we have seen so little of it.

This does not mean that religion, understood as sociologists of religion commonly understand it – as a social phenomenon or as part of the adhesive of culture – can be ignored. On the contrary (as I shall argue), nothing claimed to be religious can properly be counted as such unless it happens between people, not just inside individuals. But it does mean that we have a criterion for distinguishing real religions from secular imitations. This criterion has, however, to be applied by way of the study of religion as a social phenomenon, because only along that route are there useful points of comparison in other, non-religious ways of organizing life.

Chapter 2
The Social Trap

Your religion is not only what you believe but how you behave. It lives more, thrives better in the web of relationships than in the circuits of the mind. In practice, religions are communities, not so much of the like-minded as of the similarly inclined, by taste, values, scale of companionability and all the drag and drift of the cultures which surround them. Cicero represented an intellectual's prejudice when he derived the word *religio* from a root common to 'lecture' and 'election'; it is more likely to come from the root of 'ligature', 'league', and 'legal'. For most practitioners, it is about ties that bind you into a society, rather than thoughts you have in your head. The future of religion depends, therefore, not so much on the progress of science or the rise of scepticism or the corrosion of doubt as on how society goes on changing.

Catholics are not Catholics, for example, because they believe all or any of the forty dogmas of the faith. Most are unable to remember them, if they were ever taught them in the first place. But they hunger and thirst for the sacraments – the rites by which divine grace is mediated. Most Orthodox could not tell you the difference between the Procession of the Holy Spirit and the Consubstantiality of the Son if these delicacies were served up with watercress. But they love the sense of belonging to a communion of numinous worship, universal claims and reassuring antiquity. Early Protestants were fired by the experience of vernacular services and congregational participation. Their rebellion against Rome was not defined, as so many historians define it, doctrinally: by Luther's belief in man's helplessness to contribute to his own salvation in competition with God. This doctrine of 'justification by faith' was part of Catholic tradition anyway.

All but a few traditional Christian Churches share a creed which states that 'no man can be saved' unless he believes that 'three incomprehensibles are not three incomprehensibles but one incomprehensible'. The effect of this clause in the creed of St Athanasius is to take belief, in most normal senses of the word, out of the act of Christian commitment altogether. In the context, 'belief' in such a nebulous formula can only mean willingness to say it, without being able to grasp it intellectually. It is an act rather than a belief that is demanded – an act of submission to higher wisdom and of conformity to a community. Christianity obeys the sociology of the Spanish proverb: 'Tell me whom you walk with and I will tell you who you are.' So do most religions.

Judaism, Islam and Buddhism, with Christianity, are the religions whose adherents are most likely to repudiate this suggestion. All of them were founded in reaction against religions of ritual – the superstitions of pagans who thought their relationships with transcendent beings depended on acts of appeasement and divine payola. Jews, Christians, Muslims and Buddhists, by contrast, emphasized the prior necessity of the right state of mind. All these faiths have been prolific in formulating rival orthodoxies and minatory demands for 'correct belief'. Yet all slide back into the temptation to judge people by outward signs – the gestures, speech-arts, cringings, abasements, ablutions, body language, parades and displays by which members of a community recognize each other.

Judaism seems to have more to do with how you are identified than what you believe. Conversions can happen but Jews generally admit each other to shared identity by birthright, which has nothing to do with belief. They exclude each other from their rival sects according to criteria of ritual observance and way of life. Their religion can be defined as reverence for a particular body of tradition – the 'Law and the Prophets' – which prescribes a practical civil code and a programme of rites. It includes what might be classified as a matter of belief: adherence to the ancient Hebrew concept of a supreme being as a universal creator who made everything from nothing, a stern judge of mankind according to the criterion of righteousness, a tribal god of a 'chosen people' and a cosmic provider with an elusive plan for the whole of creation. Now, however, other religions have pillaged this concept: it has become part of the booty of the ravaged Temple. It no longer distinguishes Jews, whose sense of Jewishness is forged instead by the terrible memory of a unique 'sacred history' of common suffering and fellow feeling.

Islam was proclaimed by its founder as a state of life, not just a system of belief. That is what 'Islam' means – literally, resignation or self-surrender. In contrast with Christ, whose social prescriptions seemed defiantly unpractical, Muhammad devised a blueprint for an invincibly efficient society. He discarded the tribal model, which had kept Arabs divided, and substituted allegiance to the person of the Prophet and his successors. Today that loyalty has become problematic. No convincing successor exists and submission is transferred to pretenders or diffused among the 'community of the faithful'. In the early days, however, when the 'commander of the faithful' really was a general in a holy war, Muslim unity resembled military discipline. Once mobilized, Islam could not be stopped until, less than a hundred years after the Prophet's death, it had reached out of the remote corner of Arabia where it began, to the walls of Constantinople and the ramparts of the Cantabrian mountains.

Muhammad enjoined a realistic marriage code – up to four wives, easy divorce. By the standards of the time, this represented a demanding level of continence but it seems relaxed compared with Christ's requirement of lifelong monogamy, with celibacy as the only alternative. The Prophet also called for a socially useful, individually beneficial routine of fasting, alms-giving and prayer. He specified tough regulations for dealing with enemies or criminals and benign practices for slaves, orphans, widows and the weak and oppressed. Rites were distinctive enough to declare a new dispensation yet conformable to the religious traditions of the region: pagans would recognize the veneration of the black rock of Mecca; Jews would sympathize with circumcision as an initiation procedure; Christians would notice the scriptural resonances in recitations of the Quran. The formula Muslims repeat as a proclamation of Islamic identity is a statement of belief in no god but God and Muhammad as his Prophet. But its utterance is a ritual. What defines the Muslim as Muslim is the ritual act, not his private opinion of its content.

Buddhism has a creed which all adherents are supposed to accept. The beliefs it specifies, however, amount to confidence in a programme of conduct – pain obliterated by the annihilation of craving. All other tracks in the 'right path' reduce to aspects of behaviour: speech, action, way of life, effort, consistency, concentration. Indeed, Buddhism is so weak in beliefs that some people, including Buddhists, want to deny that it is a religion at all. According to tradition, Buddha refused to commit himself, in dialogue with disciples, on questions generally considered fundamental to a religious understanding of the cosmos, such as whether God exists, whether heaven exists, whether the universe was created, whether the soul is separable from the body and whether there are other worlds than ours.

Religious behaviour differs from secular behaviour not because it involves belief but because it is linked with committed attitudes to transcendence. But, if such an attitude is a defining characteristic of religion, we should not be surprised if, like many defining characteristics, it gets left out of account, marginalized or forgotten. No one who draws a line on a page or paints one on a billboard or a pitch allows himself to be influenced by the definition of a line as length without magnitude. No one calculates metres in awareness of the stick in Paris that defines their dimensions. Lovers do not trouble about the definition of love, if there is one; nor artists about that of art, except when their inspiration withers. Religious people usually go through their observances without sparing much thought for God. Those whose religion is residual or distracted by worldly priorities, often remember their basic attitude only on the brink of death, like Lord Marchmain, resisting religion and defying extinction with the same tenacity, but summoning his last strength to make the sign of the cross.

The sense of transcendence distinguishes the sacred from the profane. But we should not expect religions to be unaware of the world. The sense of transcendence is an addition to a worldly perspective, not a substitute for it. If heaven exists, the world is enclosed by it. If there are other universes than ours, ours forms part of the array of them. The here-and-now is part of the universal and everlasting. The future of religion, if there is one, will happen in the world we know. The problem is one of balance. When religions become absorbed with the world, they cease to be religions. When they ignore it, they cease to be effective.

Chapter 3
The Glutinous World

It is hard for this world to compete with others. We know it too well. When we imagine a better one, we start with the defects of the world we already have.

As a result, religions tend to acquire an other-worldly look. Their objectives seem focused on an afterlife or a kind of parallel universe called heaven. They proclaim standards of perfection unattainable in the confines of the flesh and the realm of the devil. Seekers after an earthly paradise are not considered religious in the same sense; we call them social utopians, for instance, or Marxists or Nazis or some such name. When the clergy want religious inspiration to be employed to make our world better, politicians accuse them of interfering outside their sphere.

Yet matter and spirit, for most people, for most of the time, have been mutually charged, thoroughly interpenetrated or inseparably fused. States and faiths have always corrupted each other. The pretence of religion has been politically exploited, to justify wars and terrorism, to impose social ethics, to bolster elites or legitimate revolutions, to sanctify authority or subvert it. Most ways of life which their adherents represented as religion have been this-worldly, more concerned with satisfaction or survival in this world than with salvation in the next. Rites directed to the afterlife are normally postponed in favour of the more urgent demands of the next rains or floods or harvest.

Even in a religion of fairly recent origin, like Christianity, which is hardly 2,000 years old, and which might therefore be supposed to be relatively sophisticated, godly elites have had to make continual concessions to the earthy, earthly priorities of under-evangelized masses. Common people's prayers are for good weather or good hunting and good cheer – things you need well in advance of the next world. In nominally Christian countrysides, the sacrament is abused as a talisman against hostile nature – drought, say, or plagues of insects – and the feasts of saints are treated as acts of propitiation to influence the weather or hold pestilence at bay. Worldliness has made durable intrusions in the Christian calendar. Urban churches, where congregations are well protected by modern technology from failures of the harvest elsewhere, still have their harvest festivals, when altars are laden with marrows from the supermarket or with 'home' produce cooked up out of shop-bought ingredients. Christmas, Epiphany, Easter and Lent are all survivals from the ritual calendars of paganism, determined by the rhythm of the seasons and the vital cycle of the sunshine.

Considered from one point of view, the movements we call the 'Reformation' and the 'Counter-Reformation' were a common war of divines against popular culture, an attempt to wean on to a spiritual diet lives permanently threatened by natural disaster. Trials of rats and exorcisms of locusts, appeals to folk-healers and wise-women, vows to saints for worldly purposes, charms to master nature and spells to conjure the occult – these were the shared enemies whom the clergy of all Christian traditions strove to control or curtail. The clergy set out to make the rough places plain but most of the familiar, irrational bumps in the rural landscape survived the epoch of reform.

Religion stayed where it had always been – in the community rather than the Church. Everywhere, devotion ticked away to the time-scale of the countryside, with feasts and fasts adjusted to the oscillations of dearth and glut. Industrialization and urbanization have shifted religious priorities out of the furrows and penfolds, but not out of this world. Every week I hear the bidding prayers of ordinary people. When they mention peace, it is peace in Bosnia or Ulster or some other earth-bound place. When they speak of health, it is usually of the body. They pray for graces rather than grace, succour or solace for the victims of modern life – the homeless, the elderly, the poor, the prey and perpetrators of crime, the work-stressed and the examination candidates. Except in cases of bereavement, heaven hardly gets mentioned. When I have finished hearing the voices of the faithful, I read the views of Christian intellectuals. Their weeklies are full of social Christianity. They spend far more time suggesting improvements to this world than making provision for the next. Up to a point, this all seems appropriate. Christianity is trapped in anxieties for the earth by the veneration of a god who chose to live in it.

In my favourite painting of Christ, Murillo makes him a naughty boy. The infant Jesus is treating a pet bird badly, gripping it tightly, waggling it aloft to tease the family dog. Mary and Joseph interfere with the typical resolve of parents: reproofs tempered by indulgence. According to Catholic orthodoxy, the human Christ was 'a man like us in all things but sin' and the painting escapes the charge of heresy only because the naughtiness of a child can be considered unsinful. It is engaging, however, precisely because it is so perilous, edging round heresy by a delicate margin. The idea of a god so human that his parents have to teach him to be good heightens the convincing paradox of the faith. Murillo's mischievous *gamin* makes an invigorating change from the anodyne Christchild commonly depicted – so good that he seems inhuman, so untouched by temptation that he seems detached from the world. Unless invested with the kind of sympathetic humanity Murillo gives him, he might as well have stayed in heaven.

The freedom to be naughty is part of the fallibility we ought to expect of a human god. The fallibility of his suffering – of his despair, of his powerlessness on earth, of his broken, bleeding body on the cross – is incomplete without it. Without evidence of his frailty, it is impossible to believe in the tears he weeps for the death of a friend whom he knows he can raise, or in the prayers he utters to escape his duty of submission to sacrifice, when his divine self knows he will rise again. The naughty boy grew up into the teenager who reprimanded his mother and the adult who tormented the Pharisees, teased the Samaritan woman, lost his temper with the moneylenders and recommended meekness as a way of 'heaping coals of fire' on an enemy's head.

A god brought down to earth is an avowal, by anyone who claims to believe in him, that religion is worldly. I am suspicious of the Christian commitment of all the fellow travellers of the Church who show how little faith they have in the human god by expressing outrage at depictions of his humanity. Outrage of this sort is usually prompted by speculations about Christ's sexual desires. A film which shows him attracted by Mary of Magdala or by the woman – if it was a different woman – who dried his feet with her long hair draws demonstrators to the edges of the cinema queue. A poem which makes him the prey or promise of gay temptations incites accusations of blasphemy. But, without sexuality, could Christ be truly human?

Artists rarely show him satisfying physical needs. I know of no work in which he urinates or defecates or even blows his nose, though there are plenty of artists who do not feel constrained in other respects by the gospel-writers' priorities. He is often shown at table – at the Last Supper, the meeting at Emmaus, the feast at the House of Levi – but food is a kind of matter invested with transcendence in Christendom by the doctrine of the eucharist. On the high altar of the Charterhouse of Miraflores, just outside Burgos, he sits down to a Last Supper of roast suckling pig – a cruel joke of the sculptor's at the expense of the monks, who were forbidden meat. But that kind of earthy, humanizing subtlety is rare. A variety of excessive delicacy keeps screening Christ from the world he chose to live in, with a veil of sanctity. I often think the gospel-writer had this in mind when he wrote, 'He came into the world and the world did not know him.' Those in his day who failed to recognize his divinity were not much further from understanding him than the followers ever since who have hesitated to celebrate his humanity.

The difficulty of balancing Christ's two natures, human and divine, worldly and other-worldly, was already acute in the first documented era of the Church. The gospels are full of evidence that Christ's vocation was a constant struggle between love for the world and resistance to its corruptions. Satan tempted him in the wilderness by spreading the whole earth before him: Satan knew what Christ loved. The words with which Christ repelled him – 'Away with you, Satan!' – he repeated when Peter wanted him to elude suffering and death. To glory in the world and to escape from it were both diabolic temptations. Early Christian writers lived the same tensions. On the one hand they had to fend off zealots, who assumed that the master's kingdom would be of this world and who therefore disqualified Christ from messiahship; and on the other they had to repel gnostics, who wanted to purify him of all earthly grossness – to make him unpolluted spirit, whose body was an illusion and whose suffering was a pretence or a con-trick. In a gnostic rewrite of the passion, Simon of Cyrene dies in Christ's place and God laughs to have cheated the devil. The difficulty of reconciling love of the world with revulsion from its excesses has never spared Christians. My body is so full of fat and gore and bile and pus and spunk and spittle that I shall be glad to be rid of it when the time comes. But the early creed-writers promised or threatened its resurrection. They seem to have read God's mind consistently, since he hallowed the world by creating it and the flesh by his incarnation.

Christ's claims to divinity enfleshed make this ambivalence peculiarly acute in Christendom. But all religions are caught in a similar dilemma. All are embedded in this world and yet all yearn for another. Some, like Judaism and Islam, entail codes of conduct for civil society which look strikingly like secular laws. Others, like Hinduism and some forms of Christianity, rewrite the chaos of the world as a mirror of divine order. Some, like Christianity and Buddhism, impose on their followers ethical constraints to make relationships tolerable and society sustainable. All get entangled in social engineering, politics and war. People now think of Tibetan lamaism as a beacon of peace. But between periods of political unity, from the fourteenth century to the seventeenth, monasteries were rivals for power. They maintained their private armies and fought internecine wars. For most disciples, nirvana is always a long way off and the best you can hope for meanwhile is a series of reincarnations – each returning you, in one shape or another, to the folds of flesh on a familiar planet.

So, just as secular life imitates religion, religions ape the world. Their leaders get distracted from other-worldly objectives by their sense of mission to this world and their desire to be 'relevant'. They start judging their own 'performance' by worldly standards of 'success': bums on seats, return on portfolios, influence on government policies. They have to 'work'. They have to take the friction out of the nitty-gritty of life. They have to compete with the state and with secular institutions or take up the slack they leave dangling – the human unhappiness state welfare cannot touch, the incurables medicine cannot help, the social problems for which society has no stomach. Religions are organized to comfort the afflicted and the bereaved, help the widow and orphan, consecrate physical love, help families stay together, keep neighbours from blows. They often operate hospitals and schools. People who are not religious reproach them for serving gods who permit human suffering; as if in an attempt to compensate, they represent themselves as organizations to alleviate it.

Chapter 4
The Corrupting Consequences

Worldliness sometimes girds to go too far. The shadow it casts in pilgrimage begins to blot out visions of heaven. This is how that sense of transcendence, which distinguishes religion from politics, gets overlooked. Faiths turn into theocracies, prosperity-gospels, political lobbies, terrorist cells, ersatz families, welfare organizations, alternative health-care agencies, entertainment centres and consumer-communities. In Iran an ayatollah can direct the fortunes of a state. In South Korea Dr Yonggi Cho invites catechumens into his 'Full Gospel' Church with a promise of bounding riches and bouncing bodies. In Japan Soko Gakkai can develop an equally abominable prosperity-cult from a Buddhist starting-point, acquire millions of members, found a political party and spread to other consumerist societies in America and Europe. In Latin America, liberation theology carries its bias to the poor to the point of forgetfulness of God. In Newport, California, 'Mariners Southcoast Church' organizes therapy sessions that undercut the shrinks. All the vices of worldly contamination speckle the great radical Christian movement of contemporary America of which Mariners forms part: the Next Church movement, in which some forecasters perceive a model for the future of religion.

The Next Church is a concept selected for marketability and developed on lines straight out of business school. In an urbanized, motorized society, churches do not have to be local, neighbourhood-scale buildings. People can drive in. The parish is dead. The Next Church church is more like a stadium. By cramming in big numbers – and the Next Church works with congregations of thousands rather than hundreds – pastors can make economies of scale. Some of them talk about the models of the shopping mall and the multi-screen cinema. The pastor of America's biggest congregation – 15,000 strong in Illinois – speaks of 'increasing our market share'. When Next Church congregations found new communities or colonize new premises, it is like a franchising operation. The worshipper is a customer; the services, support groups and 'fellowship opportunities' are product lines. The anthropologist from outer space, who mistook football for religion, might take a Next Church service for a development in the entertainment industry. He might be right.

Where holiness puts an altarpiece, worldliness substitutes the cinema screen for overhead projection, subtitles and video clips. Where a traditional service might have a scholarly explication of the scripture of the day, the Next Church will probably have a multi-media performance. Everything is designed to be instantly recognizable to the first-time worshipper, who needs to be made to feel at home. So the beauty of holiness is swept away in favour of the bricolage of a middle-class lifestyle: the casual-chic clothes, the synthesized muzak, the electronic gadgetry, the cappuccino-party in the narthex or yard, the 'car-repair ministry', the optional class in 'discovering divorce dynamics'. There may be discussion groups about television soap operas as well as Bible-study classes. Instead of striving to imitate heaven, the Church sinks to imitate the world outside. Instead of summoning worshippers to conversion, it prolongs their existing, trivial lives. This is Christianity as the devil might have designed it, a triumph of the prince of this world.

Rich men's heresies and sophisticates' sins are responsible for some of Christendom's fastest-growing, newest-looking congregations, polluted by consumerism, materialism and hedonism. Some of them live a gospel of worldly success, others of bodily health, others of sexual antinomianism. Preachers of the 'gospel of prosperity' are common in the United States. In Orange County, California, which became a byword for the free-enterprise magic of instant riches in the 1980s, the Reverend Robert Schuller – the Pastor Wavelaar *de nos jours* – has built a 'crystal cathedral' of glass and chrome, capable of housing thousands of worshippers who regard business success as a mark of divine election. There are tele-evangelists who carry the prosperity-gospel to unscrupulous lengths, hosting phone-ins from grateful adherents whose public confessions are of confidence in the divine origin of their business windfalls. Commonly, such profits are represented as returns on the value of donations. Despite the Christian rhetoric, this sort of religion seems more readily classifiable as a form of commodity-fetishism. It has its folk-religion equivalent in the banknote-baptisms practised by Blacks in the southern Cauca valley in Colombia: by palming a banknote during the baptism ceremony, godparents divert the sacrament from the child to the bill, which is then expected continually to return from circulation to its owner, bringing interest with it.

These world-obsessed corruptions of religion are all syncretic growths – the cargo-cults of civilization, which mix faith with worldliness the way voodoo mixes magic with paganism. This may seem a paradoxical claim, since syncretic religion is usually identified with 'primitive' cultures, recently emerged from paganism or retarded by impoverished education systems. Yet the rich man has to struggle, like a camel through the eye of a needle, to get into the kingdom of heaven. Paganism and superstition are as rife in modern, developed societies as ever in the past. The culture the unchurched take with them into first-time worship in Burbank, California, is as glutinous as that of the mission-folk of the Capuchin parishes in New Guinea, where the priests vest in grass skirts for mass.

The compromises made by the Next Church and the prosperity-gospel look modern. But religions rarely attract big followings without responding to demand. Religions usually 'take off' only if they fit a social context, find a constituency and supply a want felt here and now. They have to be culturally indigenous, or capable of becoming so. The originator of the modern missionary textbook-tradition was Ramon Llull, the Majorcan mystic and Franciscan lay brother of the late thirteenth and early fourteenth centuries, who laid down the rule acknowledged as essential ever since: to evangelize in the field, you have to penetrate the culture and learn the language. In the modern West, the culture is consumerism and the language is demotic. The priority is me, now. The hereafter only ever comes next.

To protect traditional religion from adulteration by new forms of syncretism, we need religious leaders who can defy worldly vanities and who are prepared to risk worldly failure for God. If they stake the success of their message on its claim to be true, rather than on its cultural appeal, they will deserve respect and may win adherents. When the pontificate of John Paul II began, popes were supposed to have forfeited their power to a new democratic – or, at least, conciliar – spirit in the Church. But a pope's authority has always depended less on its institutional framework than on the responses of Catholics to the initiatives he takes. John Paul has shown that a pope can still guide the Church according to his own vision and inspiration against political, social and economic trends of apparently irresistible power. It is hard to elude this preacher's spell. He is uncompromisingly committed to holiness against worldliness. His defiance of communism seemed derisory when it started – 'How many divisions has the Pope?' the worldly said. His criticisms of unrestrained capitalism may be equally prophetic. He has promoted modernization when it has meant harnessing lay power for the Church and embracing non-Catholics in shared causes; he has resisted it when it has meant concessions to secular fashions. His programme of 'loving our age and saving it' shines through with impressive sincerity. 'Get thee behind me, Satan,' said Christ to Peter when John Paul's first predecessor succumbed to worldly temptations. This Pope will surely never hear that rebuke from his God.

There ought to be similar cases of resistance in Islam today. But hatred of the West is not the same as holiness and to be unWestern is not necessarily to be unworldly. The revulsion I feel from the memory of the Ayatollah Khomeini is tempered with admiration. Like Pope John Paul, the Ayatollah deserved some of the same praise for withstanding worldly values. He was a master of the microphone and the airwaves but he hated almost every other kind of modernization. In a country where it could be said that the best way to kill a mullah was to invite him to over-eat, Khomeini was austere and incorruptible. On the other hand, his call to faith was seriously flawed by worldly contamination. Instead of escaping worldly influence, he reflected it, as if in a distorting mirror. He packaged his message in a political programme of magnetic naivety: he divided the world into 'oppressors' and 'oppressed'. He borrowed the traditional oversimplifications of prophetic critics of injustice. Yet the Islamic Republic he envisaged was a contrivance of our times, a welfare state which would enrich all its faithful and in which the necessities of life would be free. The model came from the detested West. Khomeini found it in the social-welfare programme of oil-states in the Arabian peninsula, which he professed to abhor as realms of darkness. He was seduced by another modern heresy: nationalism. The foreign policy he wanted was nakedly xenophobic, but hardly more so than that of the secular nationalism which was already well established in Iran. Still, for all his impurities, Khomeini did represent a kind of religious reaction against worldliness. Perhaps, if you try to build the kingdom of God on earth, you are bound to get spattered with its mud.

The extreme form of revulsion from the world is the desire to destroy it. Just as we can expect more and more religions of worldly compromise – more syncretic abominations, more prosperity-cults, more theocracies – so we can expect more of the opposite: movements of withdrawal from the world, of self-isolation in introspective ghettos and, ultimately, more fanatics resolved to precipitate armageddon. Contemporary millenarianism demands to be examined for two reasons. First, we want to know whether it is a permanent phenomenon, or one merely excited by the approach of the year 2000 and likely to come to an end with its passing. Secondly, we can test the presumption that religious revival towards the end of the present millennium is a *fin de siècle* twitch in a long-term trend away from religion or whether long-term predictions of the triumph of secularism are being proved false.

Chapter 5
Dissolving the Glue

A lot can happen while we are waiting for entropy. We might blow ourselves up or destroy our habitats. We might get replaced by evolution or survive in savagery – for the history of civilizations is a path picked across ruins. There is nothing irrational or improbable about expecting the apocalypse. The perversity of hoping for it seems pardonable if you take a dispassionately critical view of mankind's achievements so far.

Millenarianism ought to be respectable. Plenty of decent religions with clever, unthreatening believers started as end-is-nigh cults, including Mormonism, Adventism, Shi'ism and good old Christianity. When I got to know some Mormon historians, who were attending a conference of their kind at my college in Oxford, I was surprised to find that such admirably rational people were prepared to profess what seemed to me the obvious nonsense of Mormonism: the angelic revelation to Joseph Smith, the lost tablets of gold, Christ's sojourn in America, the self-consciousness of 'latter-day saints'. They replied that these claims were tainted by their novelty. Give them 2,000 years, they said, and they will seem quaint, at worst. Millenarianism matures gracefully.

Yet when we meet modern millenarians we regard them as mad and suspect them as dangerous. Their beliefs are not much more irrational than our fears. More murders, suicides and terrorism happen outside millenarian movements than within them. So what are we really afraid of?

Thoughts on the subject have been concentrated by well-publicized cases of lethally mad millenarianism in the 1990s. In 1993 the self-appointed 'sinful messiah' David Koresh was immolated with eighty followers in Waco. Between 1994 and 1997 almost as many members of the chalet-chic 'Solar Temple

Cult' perished in mass murders and suicides, ostensibly 'to escape a fate of destruction now awaiting the whole wicked world in a matter of months, if not weeks'. In 1995 followers of a supposedly Buddhist cult-leader in Japan tried to stir up collective nirvana with a poison-gas attack on Tokyo's deepest subway station. But none of these seems necessarily related to the year 2000. It is hard to find any millenarian group which seriously or consistently attaches special significance to a date with three zeros in it. At the time of writing, the only exception I know of is the bizarre suicide pact called Heaven's Gate. In March 1997, thirty-nine sad, ageing, 'zoned-out' computer-freaks in a villa in California poisoned themselves in anticipation of the end. They had every New Age trait except optimism. Wrapped up in a nerdish world of web-surfing, they thought – according to their own 'exit videos' – that a UFO would transport them in the trail of a comet before 'heaven's gate' closed. They even posted a 'Red Alert' on the Internet, warning, 'Planet about to be recycled'. The leader's rambling last message emphasized the millennium's end as the cut-off point for intending fugitives.

The year 2000 will mark a thousand years since nothing-in-particular. It is quite close to the 2,000th anniversary of the incarnation of Christ but – owing to an error of computation by the monk who devised the system – misses it by a few years. Even among millenarian Christians, the incarnation has only occasionally figured as a key date from which to calculate the end of the world. Most movements have expected armageddon in years not divisible – in our system of reckoning – by 1,000, or even 100. No evidence supports the myth, peddled in trashy history books, that the end of the world was widely expected in 1000 AD. Rather, 1260 was the year which aroused most apocalyptic excitement in the Middle Ages in Europe. Various prophets staked their reputations on dates in the 1670s. The early Adventists experienced their Great Disappointment in 1844.

People are silly enough to expect or demand change at the turn of decades or centuries, and the emotions they invest sometimes generate the force of self-fulfilling prophecies. But predictions of the end of the world have rarely coincided with such moods. Enthusiasm for apocalypse now has, I suspect, to do less with the approach of 2000 than with the increasing, disorientating pace of change. People who find change unbearable expect it to become uncontainable. We can expect millenarianism to continue after 2000.

The current religious revival, at least in Christendom, does, however, have something to do with the calendar; but only because most Churches are taking the opportunity to concentrate their celebrations of roughly 2,000 years of Christianity. An evangelizing mood has been aroused. Some Churches announced as the decade began that the 1990s would be 'a decade of evangelization'. The Pope has proposed to Catholics a programme of deepening awareness of the faith in the years up to and including 2000. The effectiveness of these initiatives is doubtful, however. Religious revival is stronger outside the mainstream Churches than within them, stronger on the frontiers of Christendom than in its heartlands. It is strong, too, in some religions which have nothing to celebrate in 2000, on any reasonable calculation; and, in any case, it has been going on for longer than reference to the millennium's end can explain. In the West, the low-point for numbers of adherents to religions came in the 1960s, and numbers of respondents to surveys who identify themselves as religious have been increasing ever since. In the same period, the explosion of 'new religions' all over the world and the multiplication of numbers of faithful in traditional communions in Asia and Africa have been too swift to monitor accurately.

Meanwhile, odious Protestants on the extreme right are destroying cultures and backing dictatorships in their anxiety to prepare the Third World for the Second Coming. Susceptible Catholics are being duped and frightened by phoney visionaries. Anti-Semitism is being cunningly masked as New Age babble. Pseudo-Churches sell 'ringside seats for the death-throes of civilization'. Aum Shinrikyo lookalikes dream of precipitating the end with spectacular feats of chemical and biological terrorism. Groups withdraw into self-nourishing communities of fear and nurse each other's fantasies on the Internet.

Chapter 6
The Authoritarian Genie

The new *Kulturkampf* is usually said to be between liberalism and the 'moral majority'. In the global village, secular liberalism is a tool of survival. Without it, its advocates feel, the multicultural, pluralistic societies, to which history consigns us, will dissolve in bloodshed. Its critics reply in either of two ways. A society characterized by secular liberalism is, some say, not worth preserving anyway. According to others, including me, it cannot survive in any case because it is programmed for self-destruction. Enfeebled by its inconsistencies, it seems bound to be wishy-washed away. Abortion and euthanasia are the slashed prices of life cheapened by glut. Their liberal advocates have deprived themselves of the right to defend the inviolability of other unwanted lives – of criminals, say, the socially subversive, the genetically undesirable, the surplus poor and sick. In secular hands, liberal principles become the forerunners of death camps and eugenics.

Multicultural policies, meanwhile, merely bank the blood of future massacres. Lifestyle-tolerance has faced us with the unforeseeable consequences of families on new patterns, composed of step-relations and 'single parents', instead of the traditional 'nucleus'. Thanks to academic freedom, the pioneers of artificial intelligence and genetic engineering in this generation are poised to become the Frankensteins of the next. Cultural relativism, the precious touchstone of a richly diverse world, has equivocal implications: how can you invoke it on behalf, say, of polygamy or arranged marriage or incest while excluding cannibalism or female circumcision or 'child abuse'? The heirs to our liberalism in my children's generation are going to have to defend cultural relativism while protecting us from the worst of its effects. They will also have to find ways of protecting freedom from itself. Free speech and free association favour the incubation of parties which want to abolish them. Free societies are disarmed against terrorists.

By way of a reaction against the deficiencies of societies forged by liberalism, religions will be increasingly popular as a way of sanctifying moral absolutism, social conformity and uniformity of mind. Christian hierarchs today are often in league with liberalism, because a society based on the Christian principles of charity should, in principle, resemble the society of tolerance which liberals want. It cannot be denied, however, that Christianity and liberalism have a long history of divergence and could revert to a sort of natural hostility in new culture wars. Islam, too, has had its domesticated liberals. The justification of pluralism is precious to some Islamic thinkers today, especially in South-east Asia, where the ethnic and religious *mélange* is as thoroughly mixed as any region of the world. I want the alliance of religion and liberalism to continue; it will only have a chance of doing so if we are aware of its fragility and defend it against its foes.

Societies in recoil from pluralism will demand uniformity, and sceptics and dissenters will probably be the victims of new witch-hunts and burnings. We are creating an environment propitious for a new, religious form of fascism. Academic experts have reclaimed 'fascism' as the name of a syndrome of features common to specific European political movements in the period between the First and Second World Wars. Yet even then the movements' defining characteristics were hard to specify. 'There are too many programmes,' said Mussolini, refusing to commit himself to another. Fascism was an agile insect, never still for long enough to swat. Today's fascisms can be equally elusive. We must be flexible, too, and adjust our aim as the target dodges and flits. We should identify fascism not only by its conformity to a checklist of past examples, but also by the effects you can feel: the sweat of the fear of it, the stamp of its heel. The colour of its shirtings may change or fade. The form of its rites may be altered or discarded. Its models of society may differ. Still, you can always know it by its works. The pace of change forced by breakneck technology is unsettling to most people and bewildering to many. In this state of mind, electors reach for 'men of destiny' and prophets of order. In increasingly complex societies – struggling to cope with rising expectations, gigantic collective projects, baffling demographic imbalances and alarming external threats – order and social control come to be more highly valued than freedom and human rights. Perceptions of society undermined by moral irresponsibility, sexual permissiveness, an alienated underclass, terrorism and rising crime are the fuel of fascist revanche.

Islamic fundamentalism represents this kind of menace, intolerant of pluralism, terrifying to dissenters, bloody in its enforcement of moral conformity. It has escaped classification as fascism on the grounds that it is religious, but Franco and Perón escaped largely on the same grounds. A society which exalts war as virtuous is likely to be a danger to the rest of the world, whether or not it calls war 'holy'. The fact that fascism was once secular does not mean that it can never be religious. Some of the most threatening forms of quasi-fascism today are hallowed by ayatollahs and tele-presbyters of the 'moral majority', who insist on the unique credentials of a given set of values and want to force them on dissidents. 'Christian fundamentalism' is becoming as much a political term as 'Islamic fundamentalism'. In parts of Latin America, radical Protestant sects are already guilty of trying to mobilize congregations in support of military-backed dictatorships and hierarchies of wealth and race. Some religious cults, with their crushing effects on individual identity, their ethic of obedience to charismatic leadership, their paranoid habits and their campaigns against the rest of the world, behave in frightening ways like early fascist cells.

At an extreme even more remote than fundamentalism, dangerous reactions erect fanatical sects, cults and 'new religions' – communities of prophetic outrage and moral withdrawal. As long as modern society creates internal exiles, they will flee to these alternative homes, where members nourish each other's commitment in introspective 'compounds' or in 'cyberspace cells'. Some of the fastest-growing examples, like pantheism, nature-worship and New Age mysticisms, have victim-constituencies among the ecologically anxious and intellectually challenged. Others get their recruits among refugees from examination hells and competitive stress; or among middle-aged drop-outs who hanker for the privileges and protectedness of their adolescence in the West in the 1960s; or among youngsters separated from love by a generation-gap. As we know, in the millenarian undergrowth of our *fin de siècle* lurk some of the weirdest cases but almost every religious impulse has the power to spawn a sect or cult.

Schism is like a shivered mirror. The breaks multiply along the lines of the cracks. The images reflected back get smaller as they multiply. Once the Christian Church began to splinter, the sects dwindled as they proliferated, as if in parallel mirrors, to the numbers of legion and the dimensions of specks. Hinduism, as E. M. Forster saw it, looked solid from a distance but friable in close-up, 'riven into sects and clans'. Some forms of other mainstream religions – Shi'ite Islam, Nichiren Buddhism – exhibit similar fissiparous habits. Religion is an infinitely reproducible amoeba and, though some sects perish, most manage to reproduce before they die.

Cults can start independently of existing religious traditions. Inventions from scratch are bound to become more common as people brought up in ignorance of their religious heritage increase the potential constituency of charlatans. A bewildering range of 'mind control' methods, 'human development' seminars and 'spiritual fellowships' have been trumped up in the last thirty years and are available, with web sites, direct debiting and some of the amenities of cult-life.

Usually, however, cults evolve out of sectarian divisions. Sects become cults by displaying a fairly well-defined range of symptoms. They fall under the spell of charismatic leadership, generate their own scriptures, create disciplines of their own to control members' beliefs or behaviour. They adopt distinctive moral values at variance with those of the society around them or the parent-body from which they have seceded. And they try to embody radical forms of self-differentiation – such as withdrawal into communes and isolation of members from families and former friends. Recruitment by love-bombing and enslavement by brainwashing are not defining features of cult behaviour but are often part of the equipment.

The path from sect to cult can be matched by a pilgrimage in the other direction. When it started in 1968, the movement called 'The Family' or the 'Children of God' had all the cult-beast's spots and horns. Its founder, who called himself 'Moses David', exhibited messianic delusions. His writings were revered as holy and were regarded by his followers as equal in authority to the Epistles of St Paul. He enjoined withdrawal from the world, except for purposes of proselytization, and moved his followers into communes. The early years were notorious for lurid sexual antinomianism: apostolic sharing extended to sexual partners; proselytization was by 'hookers for Jesus'; and there were accusations of child abuse. Court cases in the mid-1990s, however, seemed to reveal communes which had opened their doors to the world, reintroduced conventional morals and moved closer to more traditional forms of radical Protestantism. It may be too soon to affirm that the Children of God have graduated to respectability; but this phenomenon of self-domestication by cults is actually quite common in history. It is happening today in other cases. The strangest, perhaps, is that of Bwiti, which started late in the last century among the Fang of Gabon as a syncretist cult of seances, drug-induced visions and rites of witchcraft-avoidance. Christianity at first contributed only a mythic framework. Now Christian theology seems to be taking the movement over and turning it into something like a regular Church.

Current conditions favour cults, in some respects, more than traditional religion. Deracinated, spiritually uneducated constituencies are waiting in the streets. Instantly erected ghettos are easily contrived with a modem and the dole. Societies diffident about truth and unassertive of morality encourage value-systems extemporized in rejection of tradition. Meanwhile, the urbanizing and unurbanized worlds are hives of excited expectations, awaiting colonization by syncretist cults that can magic bewilderment into consolation. These pullulate and perish with astonishing rapidity but it is impossible to imagine a less-then-uniform world without them. The oddest, paradoxically, seem the most representative. Cao-Dai was founded in 1919 by Spiritualists who claimed to be in touch with the 'Chinese Homer' of the Tang dynasty; its litany of saints includes the Jade Emperor, St Bernard, La Rochefoucauld and Victor Hugo. By promising to fuse benefits of Eastern and Western wisdom, it attracted two million adherents in Viet Nam under the French occupation and put armies of thousands into the field in the wars of the 1950s and 1960s. The 'Vailala madness' first struck Papua in the year Cao-Dai was founded, when ancestor-spirits prophesied a paradoxical paradise: wealth in shiploads of European cargo for those who rejected Western ways. A similar cargo-cult on Vanuatu, the 'Jon Frum' movement, first appeared in the 1930s and periodically resurfaces to this day, exciting expectations of the return of the messianic Jon Frum to distribute cargo, drive out the whites and restore a religion of orgiastic excess.

Braving the stagnation of mainstream religions in the developed world, religious leaders try to reassure us with reports of exponential growth in Africa and East Asia. Much of the missionary field in those regions, however, is in the hands of radical sects or incompetent evangelists who bulldoze traditional culture and expose confused congregations to syncretic temptations. In these breeding-grounds of the bizarre, only a tentative welcome can be given to the spread of Islam and Christianity. The Catholic Church has had to disown some wayward offshoots, like the Maria Legio in Kenya with its sinister exorcism-rites and orgiastic worship, or the healing ministry of Emmanuel Milingo in Zambia, which turned into a personality cult, or Deima in the Ivory Coast, which repudiates the Bible and is led by a female 'pope'. Among offshoots of Protestantism, of course, discipline is laxer and syncretic divergences more weird and, sometimes, bloody. The often trailed prospect of a secular Europe, one day re-evangelized from what we now call the Third World, is appealing and credible; but it depends on a more disciplined growth in volatile societies than is going on at present.

Nor are the missionaries of this imagined future likely to be confronted by secularism. If mainstream religion disappears in the developed West, inveterate paganism may survive it. Folk and local religions are widely supposed to be threatened with extinction by modern trends, but they show amazing powers of endurance. They have survived centuries of pressure. The history of the last 500 years of Christianity could be characterized as that of an unsuccessful struggle by the godly to purge local traditions, eliminate popular superstitions and promote universal cults. Similar compromises with folk beliefs are made today by science and medicine, which find they have to work alongside ineradicable popular prejudices and preferences. Modern Japan is a land of hi-tech Shinto where computers are infested by spirits and where a plate-glass office-block might be topped off with a shrine to the fox-god Inari. Pharmacists have to contend with or exploit the patent remedies which inspire the superstitious brand-loyalty of their customers. Conventional practitioners have to share common rooms with psychotherapists and herbalists whom they privately regard as quacks.

Some doctors now collaborate with faith-healers. This seems equally offensive to science, properly understood, and religion, properly understood. At one level, faith-healing is a relic of pre-scientific diagnostics, which saw sickness as the wages of sin. At another it remains, like prayers for the sick, as a touching submission to God's omnipotence out of the mouths of babes and sucklings – the charming, innocent folly of holy fools. In the healing ministry of Maurice Cerullo, it is big business. In the world of holy hucksters depicted in the film *Golden Child* it is a sad scam, occasionally redeemed by real conversions. All these abiding features of modern life have the characteristics of folk religion as I understand it: they invest nature with purpose; they behold it with reverence; and they practise to control or influence it by magic or to procure miracles by manipulative rites.

Folk religion – despite its association in most people's minds with primitive rusticity – will outlive urbanization and the refinements of a post-industrial economy. Old animism is not yet dead and a new animism is abroad. People believe in material angels and demons who, inseparable from nature, patronize or imperil mankind with their daunting powers. Japanese adherents of New Sect Shinto, maintaining in a technologically managed environment their traditional mental picture of nature teeming with gods, are surely typical. In Hindu tradition, which assigns man top place as the last resort of reincarnations, human supremacy is only tentatively asserted. Non-human forms of life are reverently handled in a spirit similar to what we now call 'deep ecology': not just conserving the environment or refraining from irresponsible exploitation of it, but treating it as sacred. In E. M. Forster's *A Passage to India*, where the missionary conceded that monkeys could enjoy 'their collateral share of bliss,' 'what', asked the Brahmins, 'about insects, oranges, crystals and mud?' Scientists who think life may have originated in a chemical accident ought not to blench at the inclusion of crystals.

To the predicted survival of folk religion, there is one important exception. Ironically, while folk religions survive in the urban jungle, they seem doomed to extermination in their traditional, 'natural' habitats. Sequestered savagery is obsolete. Tribal ways of life, which survive in ice-worlds and jungles, deserts and caves, are shrinking from the saw-mills and oil-drills, the missions and the massacres. They are condemned by 'progress'. Like endangered species and redundant churches, the planet's most isolated peoples have become objects of conservationist campaigns – a sure sign of impending extinction. If they escape the viruses carried by anthropologists and missionaries, they are likely to succumb to cultural contagion. The twentieth-century privilege of studying an extensive range of human societies, with peoples arrested at different stages of change, will be unrepeatable. We live in a uniquely comprehensive laboratory of mankind, which worldwide cultural exchange is destroying.

Chapter 7
The Demons of Affluence

While, outside the ranks of doomed peoples, folk religion survives as it always does, it is the 'great faiths' that face the gravest menace from today's hostile trends. The paganism of prosperity and longevity lures some people from worship; others are deflected by the delusion that science can supersede religion. Truth and faith both tend to get submerged by scepticism, relativism and anomie. These sources of menace have to be looked at in turn.

First, the problems of prosperity are worth contemplating for a moment since, on present trends, though 'wealth gaps' are widening, most people in the world are getting steadily more prosperous and the religion of the future will have to find ways of appealing to the affluent. The masses will be able to afford more effective opiates, if that is what they want. The commonplace that prosperity is an enemy of faith is supported by Christ's analogy with the camel and the eye of a needle: the rich can buy happiness in this life – so why should they bother with the next? Poverty, however, seems even more corrosive of piety. Belly-rumblings make finer sensibilities inaudible. To think about the afterlife, you need to be able to buy a little leisure for reflection. Once your place and future in this world are assured, you can spare the effort to contemplate the next.

Though the nobility of poverty was praised in medieval Christendom and every Dives prayed to Lazarus at his death, the statistics of sainthood seem to show a divine bias to the rich. Alexander Murray has compiled them: out of a hundred cases between 900 and 1500 AD, only ten at most can be classified as 'born into a family undistinguished by exceptional wealth or social position'. Even some of these are equivocal: Catherine of Siena was the daughter of a dyer – a minor capitalist occupation. Peter Damian worked as a swineherd – but this was as a penance, not a livelihood. Early hagiographers claimed that Vincent Ferrer was noble. Wulfric of Haselbury, who died in 1154, went hunting in his youth, had silver coins to give to a beggar and kept a boy servant even when he was living as a hermit.

Admittedly, the signs of our own times are less encouraging. The leisure conferred by prosperity in the modern West is more likely to be spent in trash-entertainments, mindless self-indulgence and festeringly slobbish indolence than in serious meditation about life, death and the cosmos. In the pockets of most people, money buys a life of sensation, not of thought. Most people who do think about transcendence fall prey to modern superstitions or contemptible sects and cults. Still, a big increase in prosperity must buy at least a small increase in thinking and some of that will nourish real piety.

Prosperity really threatens religion when it becomes a quasi-religion itself – a new form of paganism. It happens when shopping replaces worship as a family rite, when mail-order catalogues replace scriptures as family reading, when consumer products are revered on the television screen and the glossy page, when the television or music stack occupies in the home the shrine's traditional pride of place, when zeal is deflected into money-making and charity into spending on the self.

Longevity is another two-faced god. It is a depressingly predictable fact about people that they tend to get religious when they are near death. By postponing death, modern society keeps them secular-minded for longer. Yet the elderly are a reliable constituency for God. Their increasing numbers must favour the growth of congregations. Again, longevity is a real threat when it becomes an object of worship. The unholy folly of preferring this world to the next tempts new idolaters into obscene acts: cannibalizing the organs of the dying, freezing them for future resuscitation and reconstructing their bodies out of phoney parts, like Swift's whore, who, going to bed, strips herself of every borrowed appendage to unmask her real self: a repulsive crone, toothless, wrinkled and with withered dugs.

Scepticism and relativism can also have equivocal effects, promoting religion by way of reaction. Religion was most threatened for a brief period in the West in the eighteenth and nineteenth centuries, when science purported to make God an 'unnecessary hypothesis'. Now that new or resurgent forms of scepticism have made all claims incredible – including those of science and secular rationalism – belief is relicensed and all things, visible and invisible, herded together into the corral of uncertainty. We inhabit a civilization of crumbling confidence, in which it is hard to be sure of anything. The vast scientific counter-revolution of the twentieth century has overthrown the ordered model of the universe we inherited from the past and substituted the chaotic, contradictory model we live with today, of incoherent data, imperfectly resolved into partial images, like a Cubist painting. Philosophy gradually lost confidence in everything that had once seemed sure. Logic, once a guarantor of truth, was reclassified as an imperfect system. Language, once a guarantor of meaning, was reduced to a 'means of misinterpretation'. Existentialism destroyed belief in the object, deconstruction in the subject. Paradoxically, perhaps, this looking-glass world is one in which faith can thrive. Of all traditional sources of certainty, faith is, perhaps, the only one which is immune from its annihilating viruses. The most striking demonstration can be achieved by peering into the camp of some of religion's most tenacious enemies: scientific materialists.

Chapter 8
The Complicity of Science

God is easy to fit around the cosmos. The problem for religion is where to fit man inside it. The expectation that religion will wither has been based on a false reading of history, according to which religion belongs to an anthropocentric vision of the universe. A religious outlook, according to this line of thought, derives from the notion that everything was made for us and that human beings have a privileged rank in divine order. Science, this theory tells us, makes such a cosmos incredible. Therefore religion is purposeless.

The process is said to have begun with Copernicus, who displaced the planet we live on from its central place; every subsequent revelation of astronomy has reduced the relative dimensions of our dwelling-place and ground its apparent significance into tinier fragments. Even on earth, human beings look ever less special compared with the rest of creation. Our current beliefs about the antiquity of the planet make the period of our occupancy seem despicable – like a scraping off the fingernail – in Stephen Jay Gould's simile – at the end of the king's arm. The arrogance which formerly sustained mankind's struggle against nature has vanished, now that we see ours as a partner-species in frail ecosystems. We have expelled ourselves from every Eden of our own construction.

Where once we loved to warp nature to our own purposes we now defer to her again, seeing her as we think our remote ancestors saw her: a venerable mother to be honoured, cosseted and conserved, to whom we are no more important than her other children. We have discovered the random effects of chaos in systems we once thought predictable. We have lit a few brands with which to peer into corners of the universe –

and they seem to have put out the cosmic watchmaker's eyes. In a purposeless world there is no place for providence. A puny, short-lived species, on a fragment of rock in the unstable, orderless immensity of everything, deserves the care of no god.

Against this background, expectations of the end of religion are – it seems to me – fundamentally misconceived. Religion is not an inference from the apparent order of the universe, but a reaction against chaos, an act of defiance of muddle. No society has been more committed to the worship of a benevolent deity than that of medieval Christendom. It is true that almost everyone who thought about it then had a geocentric mental image of the relationship of the earth, sun and stars; yet it is a mistake to suppose that the 'medieval mind' was focused on man. The centre of the total composition was God. The world was tiny, puny, compared to heaven. Time was dwarfed by eternity. The part of creation inhabited by men in their lifetimes was a blob in a corner of the image of God at work, painted by the illuminator of a thirteenth-century French Bible. Earth and firmament together were a small disc measured between God's dividers, like a bit of fluff trapped in a pair of tweezers. We are now reverting to a similarly humble self-image: marginal, squeezed. There is a lot of room for God in the rest of the frame.

Only in the compact and intelligible universe formerly favoured by science was God 'an unnecessary hypothesis'. When the universe looked manageable and intelligible, people could hope to manage and understand it. Not any more. By exposing its vastness, recent science has set itself an insuperable challenge. Both ends of creation have become undiscernible to human scrutiny: its magnitude is too vast to grasp; the particles of which it is composed are too small to imagine. All we can get at is a tiny range between the infinite and the infinitesimal. It was always a delusion that cosmic order betrayed God's hand. If he existed, he would surely not be so easily mocked. The apparent purposelessness, which is all we can now discern, is more convincingly godlike. This is how a truly divine mind would create a world: to baffle merely human intelligence.

Far from undermining religion, science strengthens its appeal. The Big Bang theory has turned scientists into creationists by giving time, space, energy and matter a single, common origin. The theory does not necessarily represent an admission of the existence of God or of a purposeful act of creation. The Big Bang is just a way of interpreting the mathematics of some of the observations of modern physics. Even if it were both fully intelligible and true, the idea that the universe began in this way would not support either a metaphysical or a materialist attempt to explain it. But it is an example of how metaphysical speculations and empirical observations seem, in modern science, to be on convergent courses. Particles of a thousandth of a millionth of a millionth of a millionth of a millionth of a cubic centimetre are still part of the material world – or, at least, can legitimately be claimed as such. But to track their movements, physics has to fill the gaps between them with electrostatic behaviour, with charges and waves. Even this does not suffice: particles still seem to turn up in experimentally unpredictable places. The forces postulated by traditional metaphysics – divine will, creative energy, God's omnipotence, demons and spirits – are not, in practice, it seems, very different from those postulated by science, except that they tend to be endowed with purpose or consciousness; yet scientists who deride the soul classify consciousness as a by-product of the chemistry and electricity of the brain. 'Purpose' and 'chaos' come to mean the same thing. Both are metaphors with which we fill the gaps between matter.

Quantum science is not mystical but it does give comfort to mystics. The whirl of electrons is made intelligible to a physicist on a California beach by the sudden realization that it resembles the 'dance of Shiva'. Science has been 're-enchanted' – in David Griffin's phrase – or, at least, 'opened to re-enchantment' by holism and uncertainty, ways of deferring explanation that acknowledge the limitations of clear-cut interpretations of the world. We are used to reliable observations which cannot be objectively checked and valid experiments which cannot be strictly repeated. We are familiar with motions that cannot be measured, events which cannot be tracked, causes which cannot be traced and effects which cannot be predicted. A worldview can now qualify as scientific without being rigidly materialistic. Scientists who deny this sound old-fashioned. The machine has grown a ghost.

Chapter 9
The Self-Satisfied Dot

Reverence for metaphysics can resist scientific cross-examination, but this does not guarantee the survival of religion in traditional form. In atomized, rootless societies with little respect for authority and rampantly non-judgemental values, religious movements could get replaced altogether by individual 'personal faith'. Before rejecting this as a deplorable future, we should admit that occasionally great geniuses devise religions for themselves which no one shares but everyone can respect. Two examples which might bear recapitulation are those of Spinoza and Blake.

Spinoza's faith was so odd that Christians and Jews alike regarded him as an apostate, and many of the religious in both traditions as an atheist. His notion of God was so all-encompassing as to seem meaningless to critics. He thought that God and nature were coterminous or, rather, that they were names for comprehensive infinity, in which everything perceived as particular is comprised. The immortality of the soul was a valid doctrine, only inasmuch as individual souls are aspects or particularizations of the infinite. The infinite, he said in effect, is inelastic. There can be nothing other than what is, so there can be no free will, no 'possible worlds'. All that befalls is part of a great web. Evil is the illusion of beings incapable of seeing the whole of which they are part. It is 'silence implying sound'. Time is a similar illusion. In the eternity filled by God, there are no successive moments, just one moment which lasts for ever. Spinoza believed, he said, in a God of love; but, since all things severally were part of him, there was nothing for God to love except himself. This way of putting it could not commend itself to conventional Christians.

Blake had a similar, holistic way of looking at reality but he devised for himself a religion so peculiar that no one else could understand it. It is still impossible to find an explanation in the work of Blake's critics which makes sense without seeming to sacrifice the writer's intention. As an artist, he had terrible clarity of vision but he began his spiritual pilgrimage with a muddled mind. His brilliance was undulled, his thought unprejudiced by formal education, so that he could achieve originality with ease. He inherited some doctrines from a fringe sect of radical Protestants who proclaimed God's withdrawal from the world, outlawed worship and ascribed reason to the devil. He was spellbound by Swedenborg, another crafter of personal religion, who had visions and talked with spirits. The mixture, however, into which Blake eventually stirred all the insights which wide reading and vivid imagination gave him was his own. He understood the visible world so well that he was convinced of its incompleteness without spirit. He worshipped an indwelling God in every man and sensed the unity of divinized humanity. He often called this widespread divine principle 'Jesus'. When asked who Jesus was, he replied, 'The Son of God ... but so is every man.' His unique insight was to see God as art and imagination or 'poetic genius'. The act by which God created the world was similar to Blake's own in creating a poem or picture.

He revered and hated all religions equally but followed only his own. Usually, this is an egotist's faith and makes an idol of the self. In Blake, however, the result was beatific. It gave him integrity he never compromised, austerity he never betrayed and charity which glowed in all his work. That charity failed only when it contemplated political tyranny, pedantic intellectualism, social injustice and institutionalized religion. Some of his battiest notions generated some of his greatest art. The belief that England was the original homeland of the Jews produced *Jerusalem*. The creation of Adam by the Elohim became a grand picture. The four mysterious 'life principles' Blake detected were the subject-matter of a sublime mythology of his own invention.

It is hard to suppress respect for genius like Blake's or Spinoza's and some people must be allowed the power and right to invent worthwhile religions of their own. Most 'personal' religions, however, are not really religions at all; to call them so is to mask self-indulgence. The 'religion' of divinized humanity is usually narcissism masquerading as generosity of soul. Worship on one's own, without the discipline of sharing, is lightly ritualized arrogance. Personal religions are usually a pretence: if intelligible, they can be shared; if unintelligible, they are probably nonsense. At best, those who claim to have them do so out of laziness – unwillingness to devise rites or refine doctrine. Believing what you like is a variant on doing what you like, the selfishness of the slob throughout the ages.

We face a future in which increasing numbers of ungifted and self-indulgent people will credit themselves with their own religions and think themselves wiser than the saints, deeper than the doctors. Three hundred years of subjectivism in the West have puffed individuals up with unjustified pride. The contemporary culture of the self makes self-gratification prized and turns self-esteem, which ought to be condemned as vicious, into a lofty good. One of the dearest objects of modern counselling, therapy and teaching techniques is to suppress all the instincts that make us good: self-loathing and guilt, the repression of desire, the will to suffer, resignation to pain, self-abasement, self-abnegation and deference to the interests of others. The highest happiness this way of life leaves its victims is the inert contentment of a well-fed beast. True happiness, by contrast, is a restless state of soaring imperfection, which can only come of a strenuous dialogue with duty. Practitioners of personal religion make a devil's pact to suit themselves at the cost of higher striving.

Most 'personal' religion is rubbish – and never more so than now, when idiocy is sanctified by the postmodernist doctrine that everyone's opinion is as good as everyone else's. People who tell you they believe in God but do not believe what established religions teach are rarely able to give you a coherent account of their faith. They are the worst kind of egotists, preferring their own views for no better reason than that they are their own. People who tell you that they never go to collective acts of worship but worship 'in their own way' rarely have any ground for their preference except idleness or caprice.

Chapter 10
Prospects of Meltdown

When religions feel strong, they fight each other. When they feel weak, they unite against common enemies. No evidence is clearer for the beleaguered feelings of religious leaders today than their willingness to 'put aside their differences' and emphasize the 'common ground'. The attempt to pool religiosity in order to swamp secularism started when the challenge from scientific materialism was at its most threatening. The first meeting of the World's Parliament of Religions in Chicago in 1893 was convened in an evacuated temple of consumerism: the site of the Quincentennial World Fair. Its aims were to demonstrate the resilience of faith in an age of scientific derision and to defend God-centred morals and cosmology by establishing a framework of co-operation against humanism and materialism. Swami Vivekananda stole the show with the message of his own guru, that all religions worship the same God under a different name. The same conclusion had already been reached by Blake from a Christian starting-point, by the Baha'i faith from within a Shi'ite form of Islam and even by a thirteenth-century Mongol emperor whose own religious heritage was shamanism but who kept Muslim, Christian and Buddhist clergy in his service. Khan Mongke's own image for the unity of all faiths was particularly striking. Religions, he said, are like the fingers of a single hand.

Co-operation between religions does have the advantage of mobilizing extra clout for shared programmes of political morality. Catholics and Muslims have made common cause in favour of legislative disciplines to control abortion, and to remit Third World debt. Baptists and Catholics collaborate in the United States to lobby for the inviolability of life and the defence of the traditional family. The danger of founding such programmes on a pretence of theological convergence is twofold. First, it is dishonest and therefore self-undermining. Secondly, it only shifts hostility into new channels. The sense in which God as Christian tradition conceives him is 'the same' as that of Muslims or Jews – much less Hindus and Buddhists – is so weak as to be not worth mentioning. If the destination of all religions is really the same, how could we reach it without shedding the differences along the way? If, in the end, they all boil down to the same ingredients, why not shed the rest of the menu? If they are all good, why choose one rather than another or why not discard them all and devise a less encumbered means to the supposed common end? If the grounds of differentiation are merely cultural, what is the justification for tolerating different cultures? And what in the various religions' current beliefs, as distinct from their supposed goal, can be said to be true? If, in the approach to their shared goal, some religions represent better methods than others, what is to stop the rival methods from inspiring hatreds and violence as intense and destructive as arose in the past from their incompatible claims to truth? If all religions ever were successfully fused, the result would be meltdown.

Within Christendom, the tendency to ignore differences is called ecumenism. Potentially, Christian ecumenism makes sense, as would any movement for reunification of once uniform traditions. It is impossible to contemplate Christian history objectively without seeing that most of its schisms have been the result of misprision and myopia and that continuing obstacles to unity are the result of prejudice, arrogance, indiscipline and unclear thinking. Yet it would be naive to expect ecumenical momentum to be sustained. The movement has already lost appeal for some of those with most to gain from it. Some Catholics are anxious that ecumenism has gone too far – diluting truth and easing the pressure on Protestants to reconsider their own attitudes. Protestant traditionalists suspect that hallowed customs and hard-won beliefs are being trampled in a panic induced by falling numbers. Traditions, traced to saints and apostles and defended for so long at the cost of so much blood and anguish, seem threatened with immersion in a postmodern mishmash which needs no further stirring.

The present situation is abnormal. Religions are naturally each other's enemies. Conflict between them has happened wherever they have shared the same turf, for two inescapable reasons. First, each represents a claim to privileged access to truth. Every difference is therefore the occasion of a lie, waiting to be demonstrated. Secondly, as social phenomena, religions are expressions of identity and, to judge from their willingness to fight for it, nothing is so precious to people as their credentials for belonging to the group they identify with.

Meanwhile, religions go on threatening each other and hatreds incubate under the shell of collaborative programmes. While they confront common enemies, the world's major faiths are convulsed by new evangelism, retrenching against each other in worldwide competition for allegiance. The most alarming, violent and potentially violent cases divide Muslims from Christians, Hindus from Muslims, Sikhs from Hindus, Catholics from Protestants, Shia from Sunni. Religion continues to play a big part in forging and preserving political frontiers, inspiring the sense of historic community, and refreshing the sense of self-differentiation from the other on which historic identities depend. Prospects of new religious wars have to be faced. Indeed, we have never been without them and there is no good reason to hope we ever shall.

In Europe, toleration is commonly supposed to have made religious warfare obsolete by the end of the seventeenth century. Yet no earlier religious war was more savage than those of the eighteenth century, waged to extirpate the Protestants of the Cevennes. In Poland, toleration was more characteristic of the seventeenth century than the eighteenth: government-sponsored violence against Protestants began in 1724. In 1725 Catholic and Protestant alliances were formed by European powers, each expressly for the defence of its religion against the other. In the 1730s the exile of Protestants from Lorraine and Salzburg inspired a vivid literature of exodus. The eschatological dreams of exiled Huguenots helped to excite the 'enthusiasm' which eighteenth-century churchmen considered excessive. Early in the second half of the century, Protestants in many parts of Europe experienced a 'great fear' of an imminent war of annihilation to be unleashed by Catholics. The American War of Independence was at least in part a war of religion, and as late as the 1840s religion was the main issue in the Swiss civil war. The Christian genius seemed at least as well adapted to trench-digging as to bridge-building. 'Know-nothing' bigotry in the United States and Bismarck's *Kulturkampf* in Germany stopped only a little short of violent persecution of the Catholic communion. Wars of religion have an almost continuous history: it would be rash to suppose it was over.

The persistence of religious warfare says a lot about the power of religion in a supposedly secular world. It may be power to do harm rather than good; it may reflect the imperfect understanding of their religions by adherents who seem incapable of absorbing lessons of charity, peacemaking, resignation or social co-operation, but it does show the strength of religious affiliations as a source of identity. This makes ethnic and religious conflict inseparable in some cases. A lot of twentieth-century warfare has both characters. The Irish troubles pit Catholics against Protestants. Religious war rent newly independent India and religion is still rumbling in conflicts in the region. Some Balkan wars have involved tripartite confrontations between Catholics, Orthodox and Muslims; the parties in the civil wars of Lebanon are identified by religious labels as Christian, Sunni, Shia and Druze. There was a religious element, exploited by secessionist rhetoric, in the Nigerian civil war. Wars between Greeks and Turks are complicated by religious divisions, as are those between Armenians and Azeri, Russians and Chechen, Indonesians and East Timorese. Those of Jews and Arabs are also to a large extent wars of Jews and Muslims. Afghan resistance to Russian invaders took on the character of *jihad*. There are movements of resistance by Muslim minorities waging war in Thailand, the Philippines and incipiently in Xinjiang. The Sikh search for Kalistan is ever on the brink of becoming a holy war. Impressive cases have been made out for religious motivation as a factor in the 'new Zapatista' rebellion in Mexico and the Guatemalan civil war. Religions which renounce the right of self-defence, like Baha'i in modern Iran, do not prevent war: they merely expedite their own adherents' massacre.

Chapter 11
The Resurrection of Tradition

To judge from short-term trends, the future of religion lies with marginal sects and cults, which thrive on the carrion of the world, and with the Next Church movement that is so good at cashing in on the anxieties and opportunities of 'late capitalism'. There will, no doubt, always be short-lived movements of these kinds which will be able to stay flexible enough to keep up with a rapidly changing social environment, and we should expect to have to live with them for a while yet.

Current trends, however, are usually deceptive in the long run. The short term is always short. In predicting the future, we should look rather at trends discernible over a long period and at the needs which 'winners' among religions will have to meet. On the basis of long-term observation, five main reasons for faith in the future of faith can be discerned. Their total effect, I think, will be to strengthen some forms of traditional religion at the expense of the new movements which are lurching across history at the moment.

1. *The unintelligible cosmos disclosed by postmodern science and philosophy will drive people back to the comforting certainties of suprarational faiths*. Many who lapse from traditional religions today are victims of their own ignorance. They think the doubts suggested by modern science and postmodern philosophy are new and that no traditional solutions are available. Yet traditional religions have been fortified by long survival in a world where similar doubts are always being recycled in new mouths and languages. New religions and crackpot sects and cults are too shallow intellectually to be satisfying, except for a limited constituency. They can only accommodate followers whose revulsion from bewilderment is genuinely unreflective. People who want to be equipped for a dialogue with doubt –

not just to duck it – will need the immense treasury of reflection built up by religious philosophers over the last 3,000 years, or at least to know that all the arguments have been rehearsed before and that rational belief in God has survived doubts like ours before.

2. *In a morally deprived world societies will need moral dogma to survive and individuals will want peremptory guidance to relieve their bewilderment.* Traditional religions, which have a lot of experience in making societies work, will be more appealing than secular solutions, which are riven with contradictions and lack the power to command assent. Terrible temptations to a kind of religious fascism will be posed by fundamentalist programmes and anyone who wants a decent society – whether they think of it as a society of liberalism or of love – will have to be alarmed with vigilance and armed with arguments. We need two kinds of alliance: between mainstream religious leaders and liberal politicians in defence of freedom and pluralism; and between religions to restrain the state – especially in guarding the most basic freedom of all, the inviolability of human life.

3. *Apocalyptic forebodings aroused by the pace of change and the vulnerability of a small world will concentrate minds on eternity.* If I am right, the approach of the millennium has little to do either with the current religious revival or specifically with millenarianism. But the 'future shock' effect of rapid winds sends the crew of our ship of fools reaching for the windlass. The assumption that change has to go on getting faster and stormier may be false. For most of human history, change has been painfully slow and the uniformity of its accelerations has been exaggerated. When contemplated from a greater distance than is accessible to us, its pattern may resemble punctuated equilibrium. We may revert to our normal near-inertia. Cataclysm could stop us short or we may learn self-restraint of the kind recommended by arguments for no-growth economics. For the foreseeable future, however, future shock is going to keep most of the world in its grip. In particular, deracinated societies created by rapid urbanization and de-urbanization will nourish longing for roots. No condition could be more favourable for religions to revive and grow.

4. *Demographic trends in the developed world will favour traditional religion.* The conservative nirvana of a world dominated by the elderly will increase demand for the sort of religion old people like. A lot of the character of nasty new churches in the Next Church movement can be explained by recent demographic blips: they are religions of 'boomers' and 'busters'. The real next churches – the communions which will have most appeal in the new millennium – will be religions of Darby and Joan.

5. *We face what can be called a 'holiness gap': religions that get distracted by worldly objectives will not be likely to do secular jobs well.* The world ought to be a religious place and religious people should not be too eager to abandon it to its own devices. If it was good enough for God to create, it is good enough for his worshippers to work in. Society has, in particular, to be saved from the worst effects of secularism. Righting the world, however, is not what religion does best and people will still want heaven, even if they get close to building their earthly paradise. The most urgent need that faces religious organizations today is to prise themselves out of worldly priorities in favour of reflection on the transcendent, infinite and eternal.

There has – it is worth repeating – never been an age of faith and only a prophet crazed by hope could suppose that one was coming. I am writing these lines on the Day of the Resurrection, amid signs of hell harrowed and the Church resurgent with a streaming flag. Yet insistent suspicions make me wonder whether another empty tomb has not been prepared for the interment of religion. On the table before me are the latest statistics about my own communion in Europe. In some respects the picture they offer is bleak. The numbers of Catholic baptisms barely keep pace with population. In countries where the clergy have a progressive reputation, numbers relative to population are falling. Although the crisis in religious vocations is palliated by the strong appeal of the priesthood in ex-communist countries, some of the most developed countries, which are regarded as blueprints for the future, are suffering terrible losses – over 30 per cent in Holland and Belgium from 1978 to 1994, with levels around

20 per cent in France, Austria and Germany. The most depressing outlook is in religious vocations for women. In the era of feminism, it looks as if Europe will have to manage almost without those giants of prayer and parish-work, the nuns.

Moreover, while almost all Catholics seem to have their children baptized, large numbers of them now spend long periods of their lives almost without seeking the other sacraments. Religion is getting pushed to the extremities of life in childhood and old age. There are peculiar reasons why this happens to Catholics: the sexually active tend to secede from a Church with an uncompromising discipline of the sexual life, unsupported by society at large. But the same trend is obvious to some degree in all mainstream religions, even those which condone, in various measures, birth control and the remarriage of divorcees.

This seems no reason to repine. Tradition upheld and magisterium respected is a more reliable indicator of success in the long term than bums on seats. The strategy of John Paul II eschews short-termism but could be a model for traditional confessions to follow. He has responded to social change by mobilizing lay talent and manpower while re-endowing the Church with her ancient strengths. Where it is unsupported by society, or done in defiance of prevailing values, worship counts for more than when it is an almost inescapable routine. If religious observance gets crowded out of some phases of people's lives or relocated in particular phases of them, religious feelings do not necessarily wane or roots wither. The graces with which people temporarily defect to secularism can still be galvanized to make this world better and the next accessible for them. The enduring need for faith should ensure the strength of religion in the next millennium. Religions which lose out – which vanish or get marginalized – will include some of today's rapid growths: the freakish sects, the syncretic cults, the shallow enthusiasms. What the future most needs is contact with the past; those most in demand will be the best-tried ways of keeping in touch with God. And the religions truest to their traditions will be best able to respond.

Further Reading

K. Armstrong, *A History of God* (1993)

M. Banton, ed., *Anthropological Approaches to the Study of Religion* (1966)

J. Bowker, ed., *The Oxford Dictionary of World Religions* (1997)

F. Coplestone, *Religion and the One* (1982)

J. L. Esposito, *The Islamic Threat: Myth or Reality?* (1995)

C. Flood, *An Introduction to Hinduism* (1996)

E. Gellner, *Postmodernism, Reason and Religion* (1992)

P. Harvey, *An Introduction to Buddhism* (1990)

H. Küng, *The Religious Situation of Our Time: Judaism* (1992)

N. de Lange, *Judaism* (1986)

C. McDonnell, *Material Christianity: Religion and Popular Culture in America* (1995)

D. Z. Phillips, *Can Religion be Explained Away?* (1996)

P. L. Quinn and C. Tagliaferro, *A Companion to the Philosophy of Religion* (1997)

M. Ruthven, *Islam in the World* (1991)

W. Sims Bainbridge, *The Sociology of Religious Movements* (1997)

R. Stark and W. Sims Bainbridge, *The Future of Religion: Secularisation, Revival and Cult Formation* (1983)